DINOSAURS ALIVE

Get ready for the dinosaur book prehistoric giants, such as Tyran and Stegosaurus, roaring back to life!

Dinosaurs Alive uses Augmented Reality (AR) technology to set loose a range of awesome dinosaurs and send them stomping across your screen in jaw-dropping 3D. Here's what to do …

1  Check that your computer has a **webcam** and that it can run the Augmented Reality (AR) software (see the minimum system requirements panel on the previous page).

2  Next, go online to the web site **www.parragon.com/bookscomealive** to download the AR software. Follow the on-screen instructions to install the software on your computer, and then start the program!

3  As you go through the book, look for this symbol, which shows you're on a special AR page. While the AR software is running, hold the matching trigger card in front of your webcam to kick off the Augmented Reality fun!

AUGMENTED REALITY TIPS

- Check the back of your trigger cards for instructions and key presses that let you interact with the animations.

- For a different angle, try turning or tilting the trigger card, or hold it nearer the webcam to get really close!

- To view full screen, click the green button on the AR window. To close the window, just click the red cross.

- For the best Augmented Reality experience, avoid having too much light reflecting off your trigger cards.

- Make sure your computer speakers are turned up loud!

- Mac users should ensure no other program that uses the webcam (Photobooth, for example) is running when they launch the AR software.

Need some help?

If you have a problem, check out our web site:
www.parragon.com/bookscomealive

DANGER!
This book really bites back!

This edition published by Parragon in 2013
Parragon
Chartist House
15–17 Trim Street
Bath BA1 1HA, U.K.
www.parragon.com

ISBN 978-1-4723-0767-5
Printed in Heshan, China

Consultants: Peter Andrews and Roger Benson
Art director: Russell Porter
Executive editor: Barry Timms
Editor: Honor Head
Editorial director: Jane Wilsher
Picture research: Rebecca Sodergren and Steve Behan
Production: Claire Hayward

Credits

The publishers would like to thank the following sources for their kind permission to reproduce the pictures in this book.

Key: t=top, l=left, r=right, c=center, b=bottom

American Museum of Natural History: A.E. Anderson: 23b
Alamy Images: Nick Ayliffe: 31br; Ardea: Adrian Warren: 9cr
Corbis: /Jonathan Blair: 18, /DK Images: 37, /DK Images/ Colin Keates: 30bl, /Sandy Felsenthal: 10tl, /Louie Psihoyos: 22bl, 26t, /Reuters: 19, /Kevin Schafer: 22c, /Jim Sugar: 31r; DK Images: 7, 27bl; FLPA: Simon Liffen: 23tr, /Minden Pictures: 11, /Martin B. Withers: 37b
Getty Images: Theo Allofs: 9br, /Brian Jaquest: 12, /Louie Psihoyos: 11cl, /Valerie Shaff: 24; Masterfile: Londolozi: 14b
NHPA: Anthony Bannister: 9tr
Natural History Museum: 6–7, 15br, 16, 26b
Hannah Porter: 12 (inset figures)
Photolibrary.com: Fabio Colombini Medeiras: 15tr, /Pat Canova: 28, /Mark MacEwen: 30b
Senckenberg Research Institute & Natural History Museum, Frankfurt/M: 20
Steve Bloom Images: 26br, 31bl

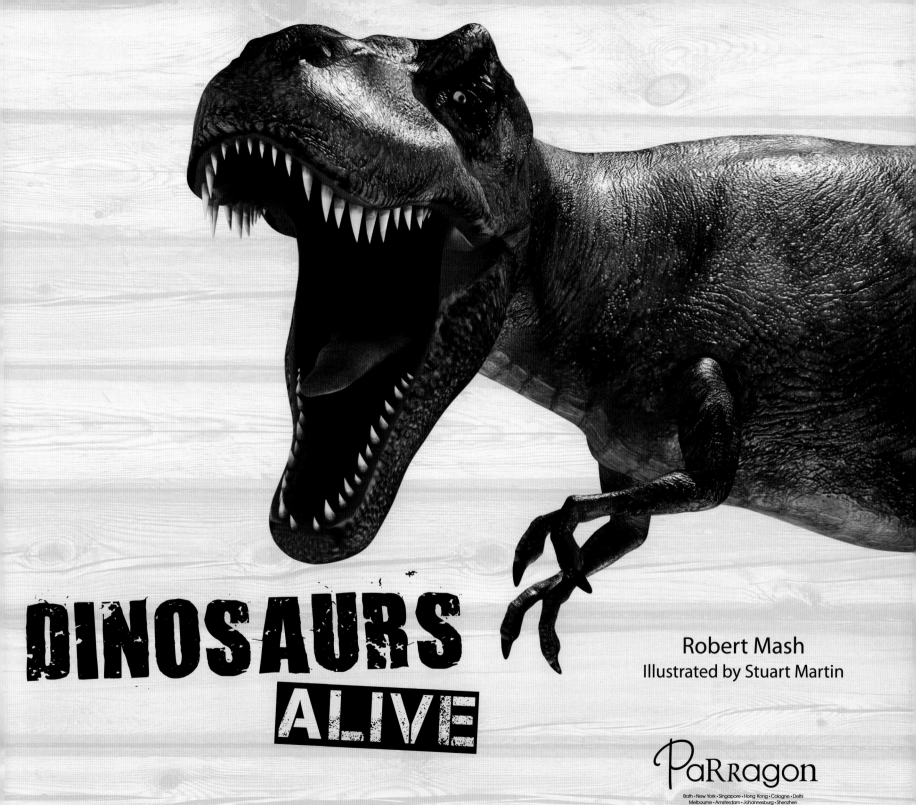

DINOSAURS
ALIVE

Robert Mash
Illustrated by Stuart Martin

PaRragon

Bath · New York · Singapore · Hong Kong · Cologne · Delhi
Melbourne · Amsterdam · Johannesburg · Shenzhen

Meet the DINOSAURS

Among the most incredible creatures ever to walk the Earth, the dinosaurs ruled our world for more than 160 million years.

Examining the Evidence

Dead dinosaurs usually rotted away or were eaten. Tough parts like bones, teeth, and claws sometimes hardened to stone and have been preserved as fossils.

Bones tell us about the size and shape of an animal. Teeth and claws give us clues about what the animals ate. Tracks of their footprints give us an idea of their size and how they moved.

By piecing all these clues together, paleontologists (scientists who study prehistoric life) can begin to understand how the dinosaurs lived.

THE DiNOSAUR DYNASTY

At the beginning of the Triassic period, about 250 million years ago (mya), there were two main groups of land reptiles, the synapsids (the most numerous) and the archosaurs. However, by the end of the Triassic, about 203 million years ago, the archosaurs had taken over. These reptiles included the crocodiles, the pterosaurs, and the dinosaurs.

Compared with the synapsids, the dinosaurs were extreme in almost every way—bigger, fiercer, and faster! By the beginning of the Jurassic period, the synapsids had killed off nearly all their rival land creatures. The only other large animals were the marine reptiles, such as the plesiosaurs and the pterosaurs, who ruled the skies.

Skin Deep

We can't know what colors dinosaurs were, but by looking at animals today, we can make good guesses. Dinosaurs would have been colored either for camouflage or with striking patterns to attract mates or ward off rivals. Their skins were usually leathery, with bumps or knobs.

The Age of Dinosaurs

Conifers, ginkgos, and seed ferns were common. Reptiles and amphibians were widespread. The first dinosaurs, crocodiles, and pterosaurs appeared. The first mammals appeared.

Cycads, conifers, and ferns flourished. The first birds appeared. DINOSAURS RULED! Marine reptiles and pterosaurs took many forms.

The first flowering plants appeared. Conifers flourished; cycads and ginkgos were less common. Dinosaurs remained the dominant land animals but died out at the end of the Cretaceous period. Small mammals became widespread.

TRIASSIC PERIOD	JURASSIC PERIOD	CRETACEOUS PERIOD

← MESOZOIC ERA: 250–65 MILLION YEARS AGO →

250 million years ago   **203** mya   **135** mya   **65** m

EXTREME SUCCESS!

Brachiosaurus

(BRACK-ee-oh-SORE-us)

LIVED: 150–140 mya

PERIOD: Jurassic

LOCALITY: U.S.A. and Tanzania

LENGTH: 75 feet

HEIGHT: 42.5 feet

WEIGHT: Up to 88 tons

DIET: Herbivore—ate plants

Why did the dinosaurs come to dominate the planet for such a long period of time? Their body structures evolved to make them fast and agile, which gave them an edge over their competitors. Some scientists believe that dinosaurs were warm-blooded, which means they were able to keep their temperatures at the same level. This would have allowed for a more active lifestyle and a bigger, more efficient brain.

There were many different kinds of dinosaurs. Some were enormous, such as *Argentinosaurus*, and some were small, such as *Coelophysis*. Some were active, such as *Velociraptor*, and some were sluggish, like *Euoplocephalus*. The dinosaurs in this book are the ones we know about now, but new fossil discoveries are being made all the time …

The Body Beautiful

What features allowed the early dinosaurs to outrun, outfight, and outeat their competitors?

- **Straight legs, tucked under the body**
- **A long tail for balance, which meant that some could run on only two legs**
- **Grasping hands to grab hold of their prey**
- **More powerful jaw muscles for better chewing**
- **Lighter and stronger bones**

lungs

spines on vertebrae (for muscle attachment)

neck muscles

LEFT: The fossilized knobbly skin of one of the armored dinosaurs, *Polacanthus*.

heart

gizzard

stout legs with sturdy feet

LEFT: *Brachiosaurus* is a good example of how later dinosaurs adapted to their environment. Instead of grasping hands, it has sturdy feet to support its massive body. Its gizzard (a muscular stomach to break up food) aids digestion, and it has a big heart to pump blood up to its head.

long tail (to balance neck)

OLD-TIMERS

During the Triassic period, the most amazing creatures ever were taking over the world.

THE ANCIENT EARTH

Throughout the Triassic period, the climate was dry and warm, and because there were no large inland seas or polar ice caps, the temperatures were constant. At this time, there were no flowering plants. In the drier parts of the planet, there were conifer trees such as redwoods, cypresses, and monkey puzzles, as well as less familiar trees such as cycads and podocarps. In moister places and near rivers, there were tree ferns, club mosses, and horsetails.

ABOVE: Fossil finds show that *Plateosaurus* was the largest early plant-eating dinosaur.

THE FIRST DINOSAURS

The first of the dinosaurs appeared in the middle Triassic period, 230 to 225 million years ago. We know that the basic design of the dinosaurs helped them to become successful. But apart from their mobility and speed, what else might have given them the edge? Why did dinosaurs beat other animals in the race to the top?

It may be that in the dry and hot conditions, the early dinosaurs' reptilian waterproof skin was better at preventing them from drying out than the fur coats of the early mammals. Whatever the reason, dinosaurs came to dominate—mammals had to wait for nearly 150 million years for their chance to shine!

RIGHT: All continents were once joined to form a single landmass.

Moving Continents

During the Triassic period, Earth's landmass was one enormous supercontinent called Pangaea.

Toward the end of the Jurassic period, the northern part of Pangaea had drifted away from the southern part. They formed two new supercontinents—Laurasia in the north and Gondwana in the south—separated by the Tethys Ocean.

By the end of the Cretaceous period, the land had moved again and formed the continents much as we know them today.

Lean and Mean

Coelophysis is one of the best-known examples of an early dinosaur. About 10 feet long, it was a lean, mean, two-legged meat-eater. It used grasping claws to capture its victims and sharp, pointed teeth to devour them. Its teeth would not have been much good at chewing, however, so *Coelophysis* swallowed its prey in huge chunks.

RIGHT: *Coelophysis*, a well-known early dinosaur, shows off the two straight back legs that helped to make the dinosaurs so hugely dominant.

ABOVE: *Proterosuchus*, a primitive archosaur, had a sprawling leg position like today's crocodile (above right).

ABOVE RIGHT: *Euparkeria* had "semi-improved" legs, more upright than those of *Proterosuchus*. The modern-day Komodo dragon (above left) has the same leg position.

GETTING BETTER AND BETTER

What do we know about the evolution of the first dinosaurs? It is likely that an early archosaur, such as *Proterosuchus*, evolved into an animal with "semi-improved" legs (legs that were more upright), much like *Euparkeria*. This little reptile was usually sprawled on its belly, but it could raise itself up and run on its back legs. The next stage was the evolution of "true" dinosaurs, with straight back legs underneath the body, such as the early *Herrerasaurus*.

Large prosauropods such as *Plateosaurus* appeared around the same time. These plant-eaters grew to 26 feet in length. They were tall enough to reach food at the tops of trees that smaller dinosaurs couldn't reach, and being big helped keep them safe from predators. In time, the descendants of *Plateosaurus*, such as *Diplodocus*, roamed in herds on the Jurassic plains. Dinosaurs were set to rule the Earth.

Coelophysis
(SEEL-oh-FIE-sis)

LIVED: 225–220 mya

PERIOD: Triassic

LOCALITY: U.S.A.

LENGTH: 10 feet

DIET: Carnivore—ate smaller animals

Improved Legs

The synapsids had legs that stuck out sideways from the body, but the dinosaurs had their legs tucked in beneath the body. This meant that they could stand upright and move quickly, and also breathe more easily. This design feature was one of the most important reasons for the dinosaurs' dominance.

IMPROVED HIPS: Hips were strengthened by the joining of some of the hip vertebrae.

IMPROVED THIGHS: The head of the thighbone turned inward to slot into a strong hip socket.

IMPROVED KNEES AND ANKLES: These each had a simple hinge joint, which made them stronger.

RIGHT: The modern-day rhinoceros shares the straight leg position of the dinosaurs.

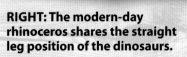

Super HEAVY

Nobody can be sure which of the dinosaurs was the biggest. New skeleton discoveries offer us evidence of even bigger and heavier dinosaurs!

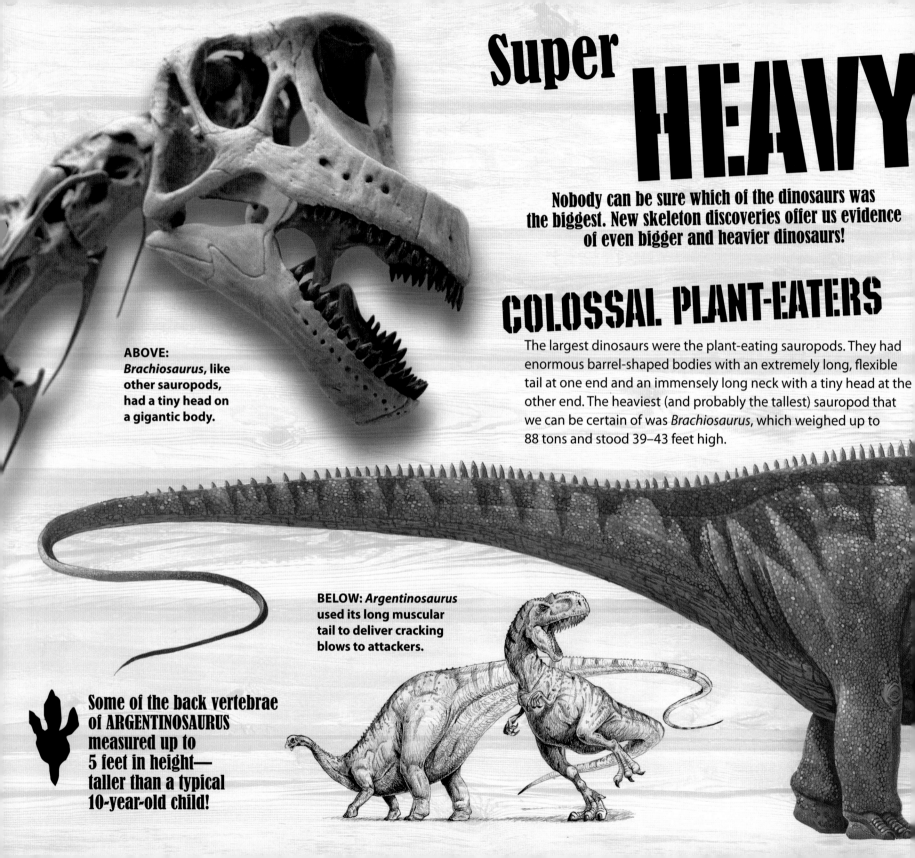

ABOVE: *Brachiosaurus*, like other sauropods, had a tiny head on a gigantic body.

COLOSSAL PLANT-EATERS

The largest dinosaurs were the plant-eating sauropods. They had enormous barrel-shaped bodies with an extremely long, flexible tail at one end and an immensely long neck with a tiny head at the other end. The heaviest (and probably the tallest) sauropod that we can be certain of was *Brachiosaurus*, which weighed up to 88 tons and stood 39–43 feet high.

BELOW: *Argentinosaurus* used its long muscular tail to deliver cracking blows to attackers.

Some of the back vertebrae of ARGENTINOSAURUS measured up to 5 feet in height— taller than a typical 10-year-old child!

WEIGHTS

RIGHT: The fossilized tracks of a massive sauropod, which were found in Bolivia.

Colossal Contenders

The longest neck vertebra ever found was 4 feet and belonged to *Sauroposeidon*. Fossils of two other sauropods, *Argentinosaurus* and *Supersaurus*, suggest that these beasts may have reached amazing lengths of 131 feet.

Possibly the biggest of all sauropods was a giant called *Amphicoelias*. Only part of one bone was discovered and then lost again. Some scientists have calculated that this dinosaur was up to 197 feet long and weighed up to a colossal 165 tons. This is as heavy as 25 elephants, easily making it king of the heavyweights!

ABOVE: A paleontologist works on the enormous neck vertebrae of a sauropod.

THE BiG EASY

LEFT: Sauropods such as this *Diplodocus* had long tails to balance their great necks.

One reason the sauropods were so huge is because the bigger a creature is, the less likely it is to get eaten by a predator. Elephants, the largest land animals today, are so big that they are rarely threatened by lions. Sauropods also roamed the land in herds or family groups, which gave them even greater protection against meat-eaters.

Sauropods didn't need to waste much energy moving around to find plants, because there was so much food available up high. They used their simple teeth to grab soft leaves from treetops. Some sauropods, such as *Diplodocus*, could also use their long necks to sweep across the ground in search of low-growing plants.

DiPLODOCUS

In the vast Jurassic landscape roamed a creature so enormous it dwarfed everything in its path.

The longest complete dinosaur skeleton that has been found is of *Diplodocus*, measuring a mighty 92 feet. To reach such an incredible size, after hatching from an egg not much bigger than a grapefruit, *Diplodocus* and other sauropods had to grow extremely quickly. *Apatosaurus*, for example, had a maximum growth rate of almost 5.5 tons per year!

The thick legs of DIPLODOCUS needed to support its massive shoulder bones and huge hips. The legs were built for strength, not speed.

DIPLODOCUS holds the record for the longest tail, at a staggering 42.5 feet.

The frame of the mighty DIPLODOCUS dwarfs a man. This sauropod is the longest complete skeleton ever found.

Monster Movers

The amazing length of *Diplodocus* has led scientists to question how this dinosaur moved and fed. Because it was so heavy, some early scientists thought that it could only have moved if supported by water. We now know this isn't true. Some current scientists believe *Diplodocus* could raise itself up on its massive hind legs to reach high trees. What is known is that these sauropods protected each other by living in herds, which was especially useful for the young ones.

WARNING!

DIPLODOCUS was the longest of the land dinosaurs. Much of its length was taken up by its incredible whiplike tail, which could inflict nasty blows on enemies.

DIPLODOCUS
(Di-PLOD-o-kus)

LIVED: 155–145 mya

PERIOD: Jurassic

LOCALITY: U.S.A.

LENGTH: 92 feet

WEIGHT: 11–17 tons

DIET: Herbivore—ate conifers and other leaves

Open crate with care. FRAGILE EGG INSIDE!

Dinosaur Action Zone

● To open the crate, press the SPACE BAR on your keyboard.

● To hatch the *Diplodocus* egg, press the UP direction key on your keyboard.

● To make the *Diplodocus* hatchling walk, press the DOWN direction key.

● Use the LEFT and RIGHT direction keys on your keyboard to make the *Diplodocus* change direction.

Tough GUYS

Even the eyelids of EUOPLOCEPHALUS were part of its armor. Made of bone, they shielded its eyes from slashing, attacking claws.

Two groups of dinosaurs, the stegosaurs and ankylosaurs, protected themselves from predators with vicious body armor—including spines, spikes, and clubs.

AWESOME ARMOR

The best-protected dinosaurs were the stegosaurs and the ankylosaurs. These plant-eaters needed all the help they could get to protect themselves against the vicious meat-eaters. They evolved a thick skin, sharp bony plates, and spiked or clubbed tails that could deliver a deadly blow.

Stegosaurus was one of the biggest of the plated dinosaurs. It had a double row of thick, bony plates along its back from head to tail, the largest of which was 2 feet tall. Its skin was covered with hard, bony disks, and two pairs of spikes at the end of its tail protected it from carnivores such as *Allosaurus*.

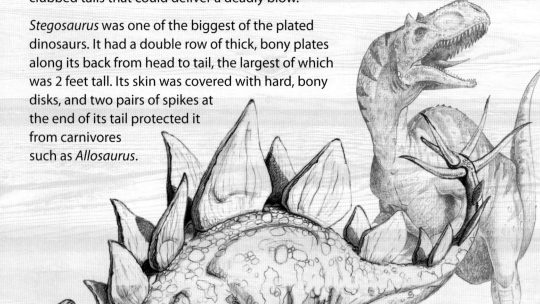

LEFT: *Allosaurus* would have risked a serious injury from the spiked tail of *Stegosaurus* in its search for food.

ABOVE: *Gastonia* was like an armored tank. Predators would have to flip it over to get at its soft belly.

LEFT: Like *Stegosaurus*, a spiky porcupine uses its tail for defense.

ARMED TO THE TEETH

The real tough guys were the ankylosaurs, who used their impressive armor to protect themselves against attack. They had sheets of bone protecting skull, neck, and back, just as bony plates protect crocodiles' backs today. Their bodies were often covered with horns and spikes. When attacked, their strategy was a combination of active and passive defense.

A spiky species such as *Gastonia* used passive defense techniques. It would squat on the ground and rely on its armor to keep it safe, like today's armadillo. A club-tailed species such as *Euoplocephalus* used active defense—it would try to disable its attacker with a blow from its tail.

ABOVE: Like *Gastonia*, an armadillo uses armor for passive defense.

Tails of Defense

Some dinosaurs had devastating counterattacking weapons—their tails. The tail of *Euoplocephalus* (below) was around 8 feet in length, and ended with a massive club composed of two fused bones weighing up to 66 pounds. A single blow to the legs from this deadly body armor could crush bones, fatally injuring a predator such as *Tyrannosaurus rex*.

Gastonia
(Gas-TONE-ee-uh)

LIVED: 125 mya

PERIOD: Cretaceous

LOCALITY: U.S.A.

LENGTH: 20 feet

DIET: Herbivore—ate leaves and ferns

STEGOSAURUS

The bony plates on the back of the STEGOSAURUS were big and heavy—but what were they used for?

fossil of
Stegosaurus
skull

size and
position of
brain

Keeping in mind that STEGOSAURUS was the size of a truck, it is amazing that it managed to get by with such a small brain.

1. BACK OFF!

If *Stegosaurus* was threatened by predators, the blood vessels in its plates may have filled with blood, turning them bright red. This might have been enough to scare off attackers.

2. HEATING UP, COOLING DOWN

The blood flowing through these plates may have been warmed by the Sun and then pumped through the body of the *Stegosaurus* to keep it warm. When the dinosaur became too hot, it could turn away from the Sun to cool down.

3. ATTRACTING A MATE

The female *Stegosaurus* may have flushed her plates with blood to show males that she was ready to mate.

4. MY SPACE!

Just as male deer use their antlers to ward off rivals, *Stegosaurus* may have used its flushing back plates to stop other males from taking over its territory.

5. SOMETHING IN COMMON

Both male and female *Stegosaurus* may have used their back plates to show each other that they were the same species.

STEGOSAURUS was armed with four deadly tail spikes. Each around 3 feet long, they could inflict serious damage.

STEGOSAURUS
(STEG-oh-SORE-us)

LIVED: 155–145 mya

PERIOD: Jurassic

LOCALITY: U.S.A.

LENGTH: 29.5 feet

DIET: Herbivore—ate low-growing plants

Dinosaur Action Zone

- To open the crate, press the SPACE BAR on your keyboard.

- To make the *Stegosaurus* search for food, press the UP direction key.

- To make it prepare for battle, press the DOWN direction key.

Open crate with extreme caution. DANGEROUS BEAST INSIDE!

Scary ODDBALLS

Dinosaurs reigned supreme on land, but not in the water or the air. Awesome reptiles such as plesiosaurs and ichthyosaurs swam in the prehistoric seas. In the air were flying reptiles called pterosaurs.

ABOVE: The mighty *Quetzalcoatlus* was king of the Cretaceous skies.

ABOVE: *Liopleurodon*, perhaps the largest predator ever.

FEARSOME FLIERS

The pterosaurs, or winged reptiles, lived alongside dinosaurs throughout the Triassic, Jurassic, and Cretaceous periods. Instead of feathers, they had a sheet of very thin skin that stretched from the long fourth finger to the body and the back legs, acting as a wing. Flying animals need extremely lightweight bodies, and the pterosaurs had hollow bones, even thinner than those of birds today. They were probably also warm-blooded, keeping their bodies at a constant temperature.

The first pterosaur ever discovered was *Pterodactylus*. It is also the earliest one known and lived in the Triassic period, 225 million years ago. The smallest known pterosaur is the Jurassic sparrow-sized *Anurognathus*.

RIGHT: A complete *Pterodactylus* fossil.

Toothy Record

The South American *Pterodaustro* holds the record for number of teeth, at between 500 and 1,000! It probably used these to filter-feed on plankton, like flamingos do.

Liopleurodon
(LIE-oh-PLOO-ro-don)

LIVED: 160–155 mya

PERIOD: Jurassic

LOCALITY: U.K. and France

LENGTH: 82 feet

WEIGHT: 110–165 tons

DIET: Carnivore—ate any large living thing

MONSTERS OF THE DEEP

Underwater, the greatest predator was the plesiosaur *Liopleurodon*. Plesiosaurs breathed air and used paddlelike limbs to swim. *Liopleurodon* lived during the Jurassic period and may have weighed up to 165 tons. It reached 82 feet in length—the head itself was 16 feet long! It had nostrils on its skull which means that, like modern-day sharks, it may have found its food by smell. It would have eaten giant turtles and other plesiosaurs.

The ichthyosaurs were giant reptiles that looked like fish and dolphins. Among the biggest was *Shonisaurus*, which was at least 49 feet long. This reptile swam like a shark, using its forked tail to propel it as fast as 25 mph through the water to catch its prey of ammonites (shelled creatures), fish, and even the odd pterosaur.

OPHTHALMOSAURUS was an ichthyosaur with enormous eyes— 4 inches across! They helped it spot its prey in the deep, dark ocean.

EXTREME CROCODILES!

Deinosuchus and *Sarcosuchus* both lived in the Cretaceous period and are the biggest crocodiles ever found. *Deinosuchus* had a skull nearly 6.5 feet long filled with razor-sharp teeth. It was well equipped to seize hadrosaurs and even large carnivores that came close to the water's edge. It would have behaved like today's crocodiles—approaching its prey unseen and then lunging out to pull it into the water.

RIGHT: The 110-million-year-old skull of a *Sarcosuchus* crocodile dwarfs the skull of the modern-day Orinoco crocodile.

QUETZALCOATLUS

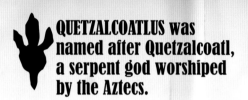 **QUETZALCOATLUS was named after Quetzalcoatl, a serpent god worshiped by the Aztecs.**

This fierce-looking giant of the sky would cast a terrifying shadow on the landscape as it glided on the winds.

Soaring overhead, the *Quetzalcoatlus* was the biggest pterosaur and the largest flying creature of all time. With a wingspan of up to 39 feet, it was the size of a small plane. It had hollow bones and weighed just 220 pounds. Unlike birds, *Quetzalcoatlus* had no feathers, but could fold its wings back over its body when it was not flying. It had a sharp claw on each thumb, like a bat. It may have slept like a bat does, too, hanging upside down and holding on with its feet.

Giant Glider

Quetzalcoatlus was not a great flier, and relied on winds to help it soar and glide. On the end of its long neck was a huge head made up mostly of its great beak. It used this mighty beak to snap up invertebrates such as crabs and mollusks, and possibly fish.

The mighty head of QUETZALCOATLUS measured an amazing 6.5 feet. Its neck was even longer, at 10 feet.

WARNING!

This strange and monstrous creature swooped out of the sky to snatch up prey and gobble it down.

QUETZALCOATLUS
(KWET-zal-co-AT-lus)

LIVED: 84–65 mya

PERIOD: Cretaceous

LOCALITY: U.S.A.

WINGSPAN: 39 feet

WEIGHT: 220 pounds

DIET: Carnivore—ate invertebrates and fish

Open crate with extreme caution. FLYING REPTILE INSIDE!

Dinosaur Action Zone

- To open the crate, press the SPACE BAR on your keyboard.
- To make the *Quetzalcoatlus* hunt for fish, press the DOWN direction key.
- To make it land, press the LEFT direction key.
- To make it take off again, press the RIGHT direction key.

Big HEADS

The horned dinosaurs used their heads when it came to protection, self-defense, and display. Their thick skulls and deadly horns helped them to fight off the fiercest attackers.

Fancy Headgear

Many hadrosaurs had tall head crests. The crests of males were probably brightly colored and used both to attract females and to threaten other males during courtship.

Some of the crests were hollow and may have been used to make different loud noises, or "songs." *Parasaurolophus* (left) had perhaps the strangest crest of all—it was shaped like a trombone and was nearly 6 feet long.

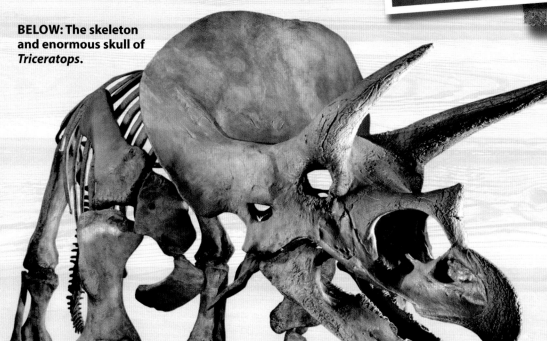

BELOW: The skeleton and enormous skull of *Triceratops*.

HORNED FIGHTER

One of the largest of the horned dinosaurs, *Triceratops* (meaning "three-horn face") used its long sharp horns as deadly weapons. It would have fought fierce battles with predators such as *Tyrannosaurus*, and even other rival males. *Triceratops* skulls have been found with *Tyrannosaurus* teeth marks in them. Other *Triceratops* fossils show scars from wounds made by the horns of rival males. Careful study of the way these scars have healed shows scientists that the *Triceratops* often survived these nasty wounds to fight another day.

RIGHT: With its three sharp horns, *Triceratops* was a good match for *Tyrannosaurus*.

BELOW: Two male *Pentaceratops* prepare to lock horns.

RIGHT: Male deer fight each other by locking horns. *Pentaceratops* would have behaved in the same way.

Impressing the Ladies

Dinosaurs such as *Pentaceratops* and *Pachycephalosaurus* used their heads for fighting and to attract a mate.

Heterodontosaurus males had tusks like a wild boar's, while *Spinosaurus* may have used the huge crest on his back to attract females or to ward off other males. *Stegosaurus* may have used his bony plates, and *Deinonychus* his long curved claws, for the same reasons.

Incredibly, the mighty head belonging to PACHYCEPHALOSAURUS housed a brain not much bigger than an apple!

THE BONE HEADS

The only part of *Pachycephalosaurus* that has been found is its massive skull. The back of this dinosaur's head was covered with bony knobs, and it had short spikes on top of the snout. All the evidence from fossils suggests that these dinosaurs used their thick heads for butting. Their spines were strengthened with bony rods, and the joint between the skull and the neck was designed to absorb the shock from a head butt.

It used to be thought that the male *Pachycephalosaurus* fought for a mate by ramming a rival's head. However, scientists have since discovered that its skull could not survive a blow from an equally strong head. It seems more likely that it used its head to ram predators. Although not very fast, *Pachycephalosaurus* was the length of a large car—even *Tyrannosaurus* would have been hurt if a dinosaur of this size crashed into it headfirst!

RIGHT: The skull of *Pachycephalosaurus* had a huge dome of bone.

PENTACERATOPS

It may have been a plant-eater, but the five-horned PENTACERATOPS had the weapons to fight off the meanest meat-eater.

Pentaceratops (meaning "five-horn face") protected its head with two sharp horns above its eyes, one on its nose, and two "spikes" that stuck out sideways from its cheeks. It also had a huge neck frill, which was studded with spikes along the edge and helped to protect its back. This fierce beast would charge at a predator to spike it with deadly, flesh-ripping horns.

Head-to-Head

Some scientists believe the skin covering *Pentaceratops*'s frill may have been brightly colored. It is likely that both the male and female of this species used their colored frills as a display to each other. The males may also have used them as a sign to rivals to stay away. If the display didn't work, the males would have fought each other headfirst.

PENTACERATOPS charged enemies with its horns, much like the modern-day rhinoceros does.

The largest dinosaur skull ever discovered belonged to PENTACERATOPS. It was more than 10 feet long and consisted mainly of a huge bony frill.

The sharp beak of PENTACERATOPS would have been strong enough to snap the shinbone of many an enemy.

WARNING!

Sharp as a dagger, the horns above the eyes of PENTACERATOPS could measure up to 3 feet in length.

PENTACERATOPS
(PEN-ta-SER-a-tops)

LIVED: 76–73 mya

PERIOD: Cretaceous

LOCALITY: U.S.A.

LENGTH: 26 feet

SKULL LENGTH: 10 feet

DIET: Herbivore—ate tough, low-lying plants

Open the crates with extreme caution. HORNED BEASTS INSIDE!

Dinosaur Action Zone

• To open each crate, press the SPACE BAR on your keyboard.

• To see the *Pentaceratops* males threaten each other, press the UP direction key.

• To make them fight, press the DOWN direction key.

Extreme EATERS

Dinosaurs needed food for energy, and they had some strange ways of making the most of their meals.

LEFT: Sauropods needed stomach stones to aid digestion.

RIGHT: The skull of a *Protoceratops* shows its sharp beak for slicing leaves and shoots.

HEAVY-DUTY EATING

The heaviest dinosaur, a sauropod such as *Brachiosaurus*, probably needed to eat about a ton of plants every day! But its little peg teeth were no good for chewing, so to help it to process this tough plant food, it swallowed stones (gastroliths). These stones sat in a special muscular stomach, called a gizzard, and helped the sauropod to digest the food by grinding it to a pulp. When the gastroliths became too smooth to work properly, they were belched out and replaced by new ones.

The smaller herbivores, such as *Hadrosaurus*, had good grinding teeth, while ceratopians, such as *Triceratops,* used their beaks to slice up plant food.

LEFT: *Oviraptor* used its powerful jaw and "teeth" to crush its food.

Grinders, Slicers, and Crushers

A duck-billed dinosaur like *Edmontosaurus* used its beak to pull in plant food such as bark. Its jaw contained over 1,000 teeth used for grinding down the food.

Horned dinosaurs had sharp, narrow, toothless beaks something like a parrot's (below). *Protoceratops* used its beak to slice off shoots and leaves. Farther back in its mouth, it had self-sharpening, scissorlike teeth that chopped and sliced food.

Although it had no proper teeth, the *Oviraptor* had two knobs that looked a little bit like big teeth in the roof of its mouth. It used these to crush dinosaurs' eggs.

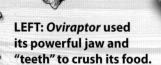

MEATY MOUTHFULS

Solo carnivores hunting for food would look for easy prey such as the sick, the old, or the young. The mighty *Giganotosaurus* probably hunted by ambushing its prey. It would hide in the thick trees until a slow-moving plant-eater came by. Then it would crash into it and bite deep into its flesh. It probably filled up while it had the chance and could then last for days without eating.

Smaller predators had their own specialized weapons. *Deinonychus* and *Velociraptor* had lethal, swiveling claws, and most of the others, such as *Coelophysis* and *Troodon*, had grasping hands. Some hunted in packs, running down slower dinosaurs. Most of the predators had a well-developed sense of smell and binocular vision (forward facing) to spot prey at a distance.

Allosaurus
(AL-oh-SORE-us)
LIVED: 155–145 mya
PERIOD: Jurassic
LOCALITY: U.S.A. and Portugal
LENGTH: 39 feet
DIET: Carnivore—ate other dinosaurs

DINOSAUR DROPPINGS

Coprolites (pieces of fossilized dung) may contain remains such as seeds, leaves, fish scales, teeth, and bits of partially digested bone that tell us what dinosaurs liked to eat. Many coprolites are up to 16 inches in diameter and were probably deposited by sauropods such as *Diplodocus*.

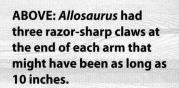

ABOVE: *Allosaurus* had three razor-sharp claws at the end of each arm that might have been as long as 10 inches.

ABOVE: Coprolites provide interesting clues as to what dinosaurs ate.

TYRANNOSAURUS

The deadliest of all dinosaurs had daggerlike teeth and powerful jaws that could easily crush a victim's bones.

One of the heaviest meat-eating dinosaurs, *Tyrannosaurus* was an enormous, two-legged killing machine that roamed North America over 65 million years ago. *Tyrannosaurus*'s long, pointed teeth had sawlike edges, which allowed them to slice through meat as easily as a kitchen knife.

Mighty Bites

Tyrannosaurus had tiny arms that were incapable of holding its victims securely, so it used its powerful neck muscles to rip out flesh with its mouth, swallowing it right away. This dinosaur could easily crush tough matter, such as bones, and swallow the fragments. If any of its teeth were broken, new ones grew to replace them. Puncture wounds found in the bones of victims show that *Tyrannosaurus* sunk its teeth deep into the flesh and bones of its prey. A huge predator like this would need to eat the equivalent of three or four adult *Triceratops* per year (or 292 adult men)!

TYRANNOSAURUS had a massive jaw with 6-inch serrated teeth. These could cause terrible flesh wounds and crush bones.

TYRANNOSAURUS would have used its hugely powerful neck to violently shake its victims to death.

It has been calculated that TYRANNOSAURUS normally chewed with a force of 1.5 tons—the equivalent of a pickup truck on top of each tooth!

TYRANNOSAURUS

(Tie-RAN-oh-SORE-us)

LIVED: 75–65 mya

PERIOD: Cretaceous

LOCALITY: U.S.A.

LENGTH: 41 feet

DIET: Carnivore—ate other dinosaurs, alive or dead

Open crate with extreme caution. DEADLY PREDATOR INSIDE!

Dinosaur Action Zone

• To open the crate, press the SPACE BAR on your keyboard.

• To make the *Tyrannosaurus* walk, press the UP direction key.

• To make it angry, press the DOWN direction key.

Death and EXTINCTION

For more than 160 million years, the dinosaurs dominated the land, but around 65 million years ago, they disappeared completely—and no one can be certain why this happened …

DEATH BY DEGREES

By the end of the Cretaceous period, there were fewer dinosaur species, and these were dominated by herbivores such as *Edmontosaurus* and *Triceratops*, and some bone-headed dinosaurs like *Pachycephalosaurus*. Ostrich dinosaurs such as *Ornithomimus* roamed the open areas, and the sickle-clawed *Troodon* was common. While the dinosaurs were becoming fewer in variety, mammals were increasing.

Why did this happen? The climate was becoming wetter. Perhaps new rivers and swamps made it more difficult for the herbivores to reach fresh feeding ranges, and so they began to die off. This would have affected the carnivores' food supply, and their numbers would also have dropped. However, this does not explain the sudden disappearance of the sea reptiles and the pterosaurs cruising the sky. What happened so quickly that large land animals had no time to adapt?

RIGHT: An *Edmontosaurus* lies dead in the sand.

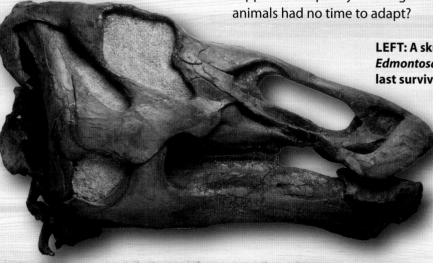

LEFT: A skull belonging to *Edmontosaurus*, one of the last surviving dinosaurs.

ABOVE: The modern-day elephant shrew eats small invertebrates, the same as mammal survivors from the age of dinosaurs.

The Survivors

Apart from birds, the most successful survivors from the dinosaur age were the small mammals, such as *Zalambdalestes* from Mongolia and *Megazostrod* from Lesotho.

Both were long-nosed mammals with large eyes a a mouth of sharp teeth. *Didelphodon*, a marsupial related to opossums, was o of the biggest mammals of the Cretaceous period.